SQUEAKY CLEAN

Jokes for Kids

Bob Phillips & Steve Russo

HARVEST HOUSE PUBLISHERS
Eugene, Oregon 97402

SQUEAKY CLEAN JOKES FOR KIDS

Copyright ©1997 by Bob Phillips and Steve Russo
Published by Harvest House Publishers
Eugene, Oregon 97402

Library of Congress Cataloging-in-Publication Data

ISBN 1-56507-719-9

Printed in the United States of America.

00 01 02 03 04 / BC / 11 10 9 8 7 6 5

Contents

1

Gabrielle & Steve

Gabrielle: Where do fish sleep?
Steve: I have no clue.
Gabrielle: In water beds.

Gabrielle: Where's the best place to hide chocolate?
Steve: I don't know.
Gabrielle: In your mouth.

Gabrielle: Where do you put your dog when you go shopping?
Steve: I can't guess.
Gabrielle: In the barking lot.

Gabrielle: Where does a hamburger go on
 New Year's Eve?
Steve: I have no idea.
Gabrielle: To the meat-ball.

Gabrielle: Where do baby apes sleep?
Steve: You tell me.
Gabrielle: On ape-ricots.

Gabrielle: Why do bananas use suntan lotion?
Steve: I give up.
Gabrielle: Because they peel.

Gabrielle: Where can you find the world's
 biggest spider?
Steve: Who knows?
Gabrielle: On the World Wide Web.

Gabrielle: Where do you go to weigh whales?
Steve: You've got me.
Gabrielle: The whale-weigh station.

Gabrielle: Where do baby elephants come
from?
Steve: My mind is a blank.
Gabrielle: From big storks.

Gabrielle: Where should a baseball team
never wear red?
Steve: That's a mystery.
Gabrielle: In the bullpen.

Fantastic Facts

How many rolls of toilet paper does the
average American household use per year?
119 rolls.

Which is harder for a cockroach to do: walk
vertically up a wall or upside down across a
ceiling?
Vertically up a wall.

True or false: The size of your brain
determines how smart you are.
False.

True or false: It is impossible to sneeze with
your eyes open.
True.

Where does india ink come from?
China.

What are the only words in the English
language that don't rhyme with another
word?
Orange, purple, and silver.

How much can the pouch under a pelican's
bill hold?
Up to 25 pounds of fish and water.

What is volcanic stone used in?
Some toothpaste and makeup.

What is the only planet that rotates on its
side?
Uranus.

The female gypsy moth can't fly, so how does it get around so much that it earned the name "gypsy"?
In its caterpillar stage, it climbs high, emits a fine strand of silk, and floats off on the wind.

How much do your eyes move each year?
Your eyes move up, down, and sideways 36,000,000 times per year.

Who has more hair—blonds, brunets, or redheads?
Blonds—they average 150,000 hairs on their scalp. Brunets average 100,000 hairs and redheads average only 60,000.

How many gallons of sap does it take to make one gallon of maple syrup: three, twenty, or fifty?
Fifty.

Who is generally considered to be the greatest English writer?
William Shakespeare.

Where would you most likely find professional
cowboys: Massachusetts, Wyoming, or
Louisiana?
Wyoming.

Which race covers more than one thousand
miles in the frozen Alaska wilderness?
The Iditarod Trail Sled Dog Race.

What is the tiniest bird in the world, and
where does it live?
*The bee hummingbird, which weighs as much
as a standard lump of sugar, lives in Cuba.*

Which composer wrote some of the greatest
classical music, even though he was deaf?
German composer Ludwig Van Beethoven.

Nineteenth-century composers Richard
Strauss and Johann Strauss were brothers.
True or false?
False. They were not related.

❖ ❖ ❖

In what sport is it good to have a negative
  number score?

Golf.

Where would you find a green iceberg?

*In the produce section of a grocery store. It is a
  kind of lettuce.*

How many potatoes are grown in Idaho each
  year?

Nearly 27 billion.

How did the first ice hockey goalies protect
  their shins?

With newspapers and magazines.

How many calories are there in the gum on
  postage stamps?

Anywhere from two to eight calories.

How long, on the average, does a strand of
   hair grow on a person's head before it falls
   out?
About three years.

How fast do the winds blow on Saturn?
*1,200 miles per hour—ten times faster than a
   strong hurricane on earth.*

3

Knee Slappers

A lady telephoned the airline and asked how long it took to fly to Los Angeles.

The clerk replied, "Just a minute."

"Thank you, that's too fast for me," said the lady, as she hung up.

Des: I can imitate any bird you can name.
Bess: How about a homing pigeon?

Customer: Do you sell football shoes?
Clerk: Sure. What size is your football?

There was an umpire who was famous for wandering all over the baseball diamond. During one game, he got hit on the head by a foul ball and fell down.

The catcher said, "We've just witnessed the fall of the roamin' umpire."

Des: Name a musical instrument associated
  with chickens.
Bess: I can't think of any.
Des: Drumsticks!

Little Leaguer: Dad, what does a ballplayer
  do when his eyesight starts going bad?
Dad: He gets a job as an umpire.

One Sunday a camper went swimming in the river. When he wanted to come back on shore, he couldn't. Why not?

The banks are closed on Sunday.

"Our canoe is headed for the falls," Tom said rapidly.

"Would you go fishing with me?" Tom asked with baited breath.

Dick: I just flew in from Japan.
Rick: Boy, your arms must be tired.

Polly: I went riding today.
Molly: Horseback?
Polly: Sure. It got back two hours before I did.

A baseball team scored six runs in one inning, but not one man reached home. Why not?
Because it was a girl's team.

"Give me a rubdown," Tom said sorely.

"Want to Indian wrestle?" Tom asked bravely.

4

Leroy & Sidney

Leroy: How do you make an egg roll?
Sidney: I have no clue.
Leroy: Push it.

Leroy: How can twins be born in two different
years?
Sidney: I don't know.
Leroy: One is born on December 31, at 11:59
P.M. The other is born on January 1, at
midnight.

Leroy: How do bumblebees get from one place
to another?
Sidney: I can't guess.
Leroy: They take the buzz.

Leroy: How do you make a strawberry shake?
Sidney: I have no idea.
Leroy: Sneak up on it and say "Boo!"

Leroy: How can you buy eggs and be certain
there are no chickens inside them?
Sidney: You tell me.
Leroy: Buy goose eggs.

Leroy: How do you spell dog backwards?
Sidney: I give up.
Leroy: D-o-g b-a-c-k-w-a-r-d-s.

Leroy: How do you make a sausage roll?
Sidney: Who knows?
Leroy: Take it to the top of a hill and let it go.

Leroy: What did the first wrestler say when
the second wrestler asked him if he would
like a knuckle sandwich?
Sidney: My mind is a blank.
Leroy: No, thanks. I'm a vegetarian.

❖ ❖ ❖

Leroy: How do you get rid of a boomerang?
Sidney: That's a mystery.
Leroy: Throw it down a one-way street.

Leroy: How should a girl flirt with a baseball
player?
Sidney: I'm blank.
Leroy: Bat her eyelashes.

Leroy: How do locomotives hear?
Sidney: I don't have the foggiest.
Leroy: Through their enginears.

5

Strange but True

Who created feather bonnets that Indians
wear?
The Plains Indians.

❖ ❖ ❖

What is a baby otter called?
A whelp.

❖ ❖ ❖

How big is a newborn opossum?
The size of a honeybee.

❖ ❖ ❖

How much do your bones grow?
*Every seven years you grow enough bone to
make a new skeleton.*

The lyrics of Handel's famous choral work,
The Messiah, came from what book?
The Bible.

How much does the average human head
weigh?
About ten pounds.

How many people in the United States
remain in comas in an average year?
15,000.

What is also known as a "nun," a "whistling,"
a "spar," a "bell," a "can," and a "lighted"?
A buoy.

What tall, colorfully-clad guards protect the
Pope—the National Guard, the Swiss
Guards, or the Grenadier Guards?
The Swiss Guards.

How wide is the moon?
*About as wide as the United States—2,160
miles.*

How many thunderstorms occur on earth at
any given moment?
About 1,800.

How many feathers do adult turkeys have?
3,500.

Fun Fact: In 1880 the rules of baseball
required nine balls to walk a player.

Fun Fact: The heaviest football player on
record was a 447-pound tackle at a
California high school.

Fun Fact: The speed of a golf ball driven off a
tee has been timed at 170 miles per hour.

How many functions does your liver perform?

More than 500, including storing vitamins and removing harmful chemicals from the blood.

Who was the only United States president whose son became president?

John Adams. His son was John Quincy Adams.

What early style of jazz was written largely for the piano in the twentieth century?

Ragtime.

How much does a typical llama weigh?

About 375 pounds.

Where is it against the law to bathe more than once a week?

Boston, Massachusetts.

In Cleveland, Ohio, what is illegal to catch
without a hunting license?
Mice.

Which of these cities is *not* in California—San
Diego, Corpus Christi, or Chula Vista?
Corpus Christi.

When was the bird diaper invented?
In 1956.

How far does the average American walk in a
lifetime?
92,375 miles.

True or false: When you are full after a meal,
your stomach has stretched as big as a
balloon.
True.

Where is the largest landfill in the world?
*Fresh Kills, New York— each day 14,000 tons
are dumped there.*

How fast did the Galilee spacecraft travel to
  Jupiter?
*107,000 miles per hour—fast enough to cross
  the United States in 85 seconds.*

Which United States city has a larger
  population than Denmark, Finland,
  Switzerland, and Norway combined?
New York City.

6

Gertie & Bertie

Gertie: How many apples grow on trees?
Bertie: I have no clue.
Gertie: All of them.

Gertie: How did Mary's little lamb fly to the
moon?
Bertie: I don't know.
Gertie: By rocket sheep.

Gertie: How do dog catchers get paid?
Bertie: I can't guess.
Gertie: By the pound.

Gertie: How do you catch a unique rabbit?
Bertie: I have no idea.
Gertie: You kneek up on it.

Gertie: How does a truck say thank you?
Bertie: You tell me.
Gertie: Ton ka.

Gertie: How does a rattlesnake phone home?
Bertie: I give up.
Gertie: Poison to poison (person to person).

Gertie: How do you catch a fairy?
Bertie: Who knows?
Gertie: By its fairy tale.

Gertie: How do you catch a butterfly with a
computer?
Bertie: You've got me.
Gertie: Use the Internet.

Gertie: How many beans can you put in an empty bag?
Bertie: My mind is a blank.
Gertie: One. After that the bag isn't empty.

Gertie: How do you get an astronaut to sleep?
Bertie: That's a mystery.
Gertie: You rock-et him.

Gertie: How do you paint a rabbit?
Bertie: I'm blank.
Gertie: With harespray.

Gertie: How do you fix a broken tomato?
Bertie: I don't have the foggiest.
Gertie: With tomato paste.

7

Duke & Luke

Duke: What three words do teachers like the most?
Luke: I give up
Duke: June, July, and August.

Duke: What is a ring leader?
Luke: It's unknown to me.
Duke: The first person in the bathtub.

Duke: What do you call a 300-pound football player with a short temper?
Luke: I'm in the dark.
Duke: Sir.

Duke: What happens to a girl who doesn't know cold cream from putty?
Luke: Search me.
Duke: All her windows fall out.

Duke: What do you get when you cross a dog with an elephant?
Luke: You've got me guessing.
Duke: A dog that remembers where it buried its bones!

Duke: What bus crossed the ocean?
Luke: I pass.
Duke: Columbus.

Duke: What side of a dog has the most fun?
Luke: Beats me.
Duke: The outside.

Duke: What, in your opinion, do you consider the height of stupidity?
Luke: I don't know.
Duke: How tall are you?

Duke: What do you give a man who has
    everything?
Luke: I can't guess.
Duke: Penicillin.

Duke: What goes a, b, c, d, e, f, g, h, i, j, k, l,
    m, n, o, p, q, r, s, t, u, v, w, x, y, z, slurp?
Luke: I have no idea.
Duke: A man eating alphabet soup.

Duke: What's green and goes camping a lot?
Luke: You tell me.
Duke: A boy sprout.

Duke: What do you get if you cross a karate
    expert with a pig?
Luke: I give up.
Duke: A pork chop.

Duke: What did the boy candle say to the girl
    candle?
Luke: Who knows?
Duke: Let's go out together.

Duke: What's the best way to prevent disease
  caused by biting dogs?
Luke: You've got me.
Duke: Don't bite any!

Duke: What happened to the burglar who
  stole a calendar?
Luke: My mind is a blank.
Duke: He got twelve months.

8

Did You Know?

How fast can the fastest shark swim?
40 miles per hour.

What's the world record distance for spitting?
25 feet 10 inches.

Which has more land: the United States or
Antarctica?
Antarctica—half again as much.

In *The Ugly Duckling,* is the duckling
actually a chicken, a goose, or a swan?
A swan.

34

What merit badge is awarded to Boy Scouts
   most frequently?
First aid, followed by swimming and cooking.

What is a "corvine" voice?
A voice like a crow.

Is the air pressure outside your body the
   same, less, or more than inside your body?
The same—14.7 pounds per square inch.

How many languages are spoken in the
   United States?
329.

What are speed bumps called in Jamaica?
Sleeping Policemen.

How big is the average adult's stomach?
About the size of a clenched fist.

Who created the Internet and who pays for it?
*The Pentagon created it. The National Science
Foundation pays to keep it going.*

Who brought waffles to the United States?
Thomas Jefferson.

When is the most common time of the year for
nosebleeds?
Winter.

Do forests migrate?
Yes, approximately 13 miles per century.

What's the only word in the English
language—not counting proper names—
that ends with the letter "q"?
*It's "cinq." A variation of "cinque," meaning
five.*

How many people are injured in ping-pong
games each year?
1,500.

What is the number one preferred prey of
  foxes?
Chickens, followed by rabbits and cats.

Do insects lose weight?
*Yes, in an hour's flight an insect can lose as
  much as one-third of its body weight.*

What government official used to execute
  fleas?
*Queen Christina of Sweden in the fourteenth
  century. She used a four-inch-long
  handgun.*

How much gold do dentists use each year?
87 tons.

Where do bottle trees grow?
*On the northern edge of Australia's desert.
  They get their name because of their
  bulging hollow trunks full of water.*

❖ ❖ ❖

What is a "bedstick"?
A smooth round dowel about three feet long once used to level covers when making up wide beds.

Who invented cellophane?
Jacques Edwin Brandenberger, in 1908.

What is the medical term for abnormally slow eating?
Bradyphagia.

How hot does a toaster get?
About 500 degrees Fahrenheit.

Does a clam have kidneys?
Yes, and a stomach, gills, a heart, and intestines.

9

Silly Dillies

Which is the laziest letter in the alphabet?
"E"—it's always in bed.

When should you wear a bathing suit to go
horseback riding?
When you're going to ride a seahorse.

Did you hear the joke about the airplane?
It must be over your head.

Who is the scariest hen in the henhouse?
Frank-hen-stein.

Which Midwestern state has two eyes but
  cannot see?
Indiana.

Did you hear the joke about the bed?
It has not been made up yet.

Did you hear about the guy who lost his left
  side?
He's all right now.

Whom do birds marry?
Their tweethearts.

Did you hear about the dentist who joined the
  army?
They made him a drill sergeant.

Do you know how to get rid of nuclear waste?
Send it to the post office, and they'll lose it.

Which smells better—a red jelly bean or a
green jelly bean?
Neither. Jelly beans don't have noses.

Do you know where geologists go for a good
time?
To a rock concert.

Did you hear the one about the fish?
Never mind, it stinks.

If an apple a day keeps the doctor away, what
does an onion a day do?
It keeps everybody away.

Which movie shows the adventures of a
computer-animated bunion?
Toe Story.

Did you hear the joke about the fast pitch?
Never mind, you just missed it.

Did you hear about the shepherd who was
   trampled by a flock of sheep?
He died-in-the-wool.

If you were hunting in the jungle and met a
   lion, would you give him both barrels?
You should just give him the whole gun!

Did you ever see a wood fence?
No, but I saw the barn dance.

Stanley: Did you know I was a lifesaver at the
   beach last year?
Shirley: Really? What flavor?

Which English king is responsible for
   fractions?
Henry 1/8.

10

Petula & Olaf

Petula: What kind of car doesn't have a steering wheel?
Olaf: I have no clue.
Petula: A train car.

Petula: What did the doctor say to the patient after surgery?
Olaf: I don't know.
Petula: That's enough out of you.

Petula: What did the barber say to the sad rabbit?
Olaf: I can't guess.
Petula: Are you having a bad hare day?

Petula: What's the best shoe for a ten year old to wear?
Olaf: I have no idea.
Petula: A ten-a-shoe.

Petula: What do you call a rabbit that has fleas?
Olaf: You tell me.
Petula: Bugs bunny.

Petula: What do you call a carton full of ducks?
Olaf: I give up.
Petula: A box of quackers.

Petula: What do frogs eat?
Olaf: Who knows?
Petula: Anything that bugs them.

Petula: What did one bee say to the other bee?
Olaf: You've got me.
Petula: Just bee yourself.

Petula: What can you serve, but not eat?
Olaf: My mind is a blank.
Petula: Tennis balls.

Petula: What's the scariest lake to swim in?
Olaf: That's a mystery.
Petula: Lake Erie.

Petula: What do you call a buff dinosaur that
    lifts weights?
Olaf: I'm blank.
Petula: Tyrannosaurus Flex.

Petula: What do you call a cowboy dinosaur?
Olaf: I don't have the foggiest.
Petula: Tyrannosaurus Tex.

Petula: What has two humps and lives in
    Alaska?
Olaf: I give up.
Petula: A lost camel.

Petula: What is black, white, and red all
  over?
Olaf: It's unknown to me.
Petula: A blushing zebra.

Petula: What did one magnet say to the other
  magnet?
Olaf: I'm in the dark.
Petula: I find you attractive.

11

New Thoughts

Why are tennis balls made fuzzy?
*To slow them down and to let the racquet grip
them.*

At what capacity does the human brain
operate?
At about 15 percent.

How many quills does an adult porcupine
have—about 1,000, 14,000 or 30,000?
About 30,000.

The first telephone call from the White House
was made by President Rutherford B.
Hayes in 1878. Who did he call?
Alexander Graham Bell.

In what state is it illegal to whistle
underwater?
Vermont.

What is the hardest natural substance in the
world?
A diamond.

On what day are the most potato chips sold?
*On Super Bowl day. Sales go up an extra 150
million bags, according to Frito-Lay.*

Which has more vitamin C—strawberries or
oranges?
Strawberries.

What is the record for yo-yo endurance?
8 hours, 32 minutes.

48

Why is Britain's main monetary unit called a
   "pound"?
Its value once equaled a pound of silver.

Were the ancient Romans vegetarians?
Yes, until Caesar took over.

What is the longest recorded time a person
   has been able to stay underwater and live
   to tell about it?
13 minutes and 42.5 seconds.

The largest ocean in the world is the Pacific
   Ocean. Which ocean is second largest?
The Atlantic Ocean.

Aesop, known for his fables, lived from 620 to
   560 B.C. in what country?
Greece.

True or false: One in four Americans have appeared on television.
True.

Where did Panama hats originate?
Ecuador.

What element has the most reported uses?
Salt, which has 14,000 industrial uses.

In how many different languages could you play Monopoly?
25 different languages.

How sensitive is the sonar of bats?
They are able to dodge wires only slightly thicker than a human hair.

How many lightning bolts snap, crackle, and pop in the earth's atmosphere?
100 per second.

50

What state in the United States has a law
that makes it a crime to bathe less than
once per year?
Kentucky.

Who was the first person to use a parachute?
*André Jacques Garnerin—in 1797. He jumped
out of a hot air balloon at 2,230 feet.*

How many revolutions has the planet
Neptune completed since it was discovered
in 1846?
Only about ¾ of one.

How much power does the typical toaster use?
1,100 watts.

What is the average attention span while
listening to somebody else talk?
Eight seconds.

Where did the first roses grow?
In the ancient Middle East.

12

Tony & Tobiah

Tony: Why did the glass container go to
  Hollywood?
Tobiah: I have no clue.
Tony: She wanted to be a movie jar.

Tony: Why can't a bicycle stand by itself?
Tobiah: I don't know.
Tony: Because it's two tired.

Tony: Why shouldn't you tell a secret to a pig?
Tobiah: I can't guess.
Tony: Because it will squeal on you.

Tony: Why is a math book always cranky?
Tobiah: I have no idea.
Tony: Because it has lots of problems.

Tony: Why did the man climb to the roof of
the restaurant?
Tobiah: You tell me.
Tony: They told him the meal was on the
house.

Tony: Why did the skeleton fail first grade?
Tobiah: I give up.
Tony: Because he was a bonehead.

Tony: Why doesn't a car get cold?
Tobiah: Who knows?
Tony: Because it has a muffler.

Tony: Why couldn't the pony talk?
Tobiah: You've got me.
Tony: Because he was a little horse.

Tony: Why does a lion wear a thick fur coat?
Tobiah: My mind is a blank.
Tony: Because he'd look stupid in a plastic
raincoat.

Tony: Why did the hen lay an egg?
Tobiah: That's a mystery.
Tony: Because if she dropped it, it would
break.

Tony: Why is it hard for a ladybug to hide?
Tobiah: I'm blank.
Tony: Because she is always spotted.

Tony: Why did the orange stop in the middle
of the road?
Tobiah: I don't have the foggiest.
Tony: Because it ran out of juice.

Tony: Why do bees have sticky hair?
Tobiah: I give up.
Tony: Because they use a honeycomb.

Tony: Why did the man wear three jackets
while painting?
Tobiah: It's unknown to me.
Tony: The directions on the paint can said to
put on three coats.

Tony: Why did the girl tiptoe past the tents?
Tobiah: I'm in the dark.
Tony: She didn't want to wake up the sleeping
bags.

13

Vito & Oliver

Vito: What's a cat's favorite color?
Oliver: I have no clue.
Vito: Purrrr-ple.

Vito: What's the best place to shop for a soccer
shirt?
Oliver: I don't know.
Vito: New Jersey.

Vito: What do you get if you cross a gopher
and a porcupine?
Oliver: I can't guess.
Vito: A tunnel that leaks.

Vito: Imagine a tiger was chasing you. What would you do?

Oliver: I have no idea.

Vito: Quit imagining.

Vito: What is the beginning of eternity, the end of time and space, the beginning of every end and the end of every place?

Oliver: You tell me.

Vito: The letter "e."

Vito: What kind of dog has no legs?

Oliver: I give up.

Vito: A hot dog.

Vito: What would you get if you crossed a rooster with a duck?

Oliver: Who knows.

Vito: The kind of animal that wakes people up at the quack of dawn. Quack! Quack!

Vito: What would you get if you crossed a cocker spaniel, a French poodle, and a ghost?

Oliver: You've got me.

Vito: A cocker-poodle-boo!

❖ ❖ ❖

Vito: What do you call a black dog that has been in the sun?

Oliver: My mind is a blank.

Vito: A hot dog.

❖ ❖ ❖

Vito: What's smarter than a talking parrot?

Oliver: That's a mystery.

Vito: A spelling bee.

❖ ❖ ❖

Vito: What kind of a horse makes a really good friend?

Oliver: I'm blank.

Vito: A pal-o-mino.

❖ ❖ ❖

Vito: What do you call a bee who buzzes very quietly?

Oliver: I don't have the foggiest.

Vito: A mumble bee.

Vito: What did the digital watch say to its
  mother?
Oliver: I give up.
Vito: Look, Ma, no hands.

Vito: What does an invisible cat drink?
Oliver: It's unknown to me.
Vito: Evaporated milk.

Vito: What do you call a person who lives next
  door to a tiger?
Oliver: I'm in the dark.
Vito: A tasty midnight snack.

14

Tell a Friend

Was Vermont one of the original 13 colonies?
No, it was state number 14.

Which is warmer—the Arctic Ocean or the
   Antarctic Ocean?
The Arctic Ocean—by ten degrees.

What is a "woolly bear"?
A caterpillar.

Who suffers the most on-the-job injuries—
   garbagemen, policemen, or firemen?
Garbagemen.

How long does a taste bud usually survive —
   five minutes, an hour, or a few days?

A few days.

United States grain consumption has gone up
   100 percent since the 1970s. Why?

*Pizza, pasta, and Mexican food have become
   more popular foods in the United States.*

How big were most dinosaurs?

The size of chickens.

What are four different places where you can
   play a game of hockey?

*On a field, on ice, underwater, or on a roller
   rink.*

How do some mantis shrimp travel?

By doing backward somersaults.

How many hot dogs are eaten each year
worldwide?
*14 billion— enough links to stretch to the
moon and back three times.*

How many rivers in the United States are
more than 100 miles long?
135.

How often does the human heart beat each
year?
40 million times.

How much do lions sleep?
Up to 20 hours per day.

How much do your ears grow?
About .0087 of an inch each year.

What is the fastest land animal in the world?
*The cheetah, which can run up to 62 miles per
hour.*

Which has more muscles in their body—a
  human or a caterpillar?
*Caterpillars, which have 4,000. Humans have
  only 639 muscles.*

How much of an iceberg can be seen above
  water?
Only about 12 percent; the rest is underwater.

What state is known as the Land of Lincoln?
Illinois.

On what day of the year are the most collect
  calls made?
Father's Day.

What gives silk its beautiful sheen?
*Its fibers are triangular, so they reflect light as
  prisms.*

What makes goldfish stay small in a bowl but
grow bigger in a pond?
*They secrete a substance that inhibits growth
when it is concentrated but doesn't when
diluted.*

What did knights of old call a shield that
protected the entire body?
A pavis.

What does a "limnologist" study?
Lakes.

Can male and female cockatoos be taught to
talk?
Only the male. The female chirps and sings.

How much does a cricket eat each day?
As much as it weighs.

Hoarse Laughs

Name a chicken holiday.
April Fowl's Day!

Name a famous chicken explorer.
Admiral Bird!

First Wrestler: Want to see something really
  swell?
Second Wrestler: Sure.
First Wrestler: Hit yourself on the head with
  a baseball bat.

Father: Bonnie, please take the dog out and give him some air.

Bonnie: Sure, Dad. Where is the nearest gas station?

In filling out an application for a factory job, a man was puzzled for a long time over a question: "Person to notify in case of emergency." Finally he wrote: "Anybody in sight."

Teachers do not retire, they just lose their faculties.

As you walk in the Internal Revenue Service there's a sign that says, "Watch your step." As you exit there is another sign that says, "Watch your mouth."

My dog's name is Camera. He snaps a lot.

When I was little I was the teacher's pet. She could not find a dog.

If a carrot and a cabbage run a race, which one would win?
The cabbage, because it's ahead.

If the Smurfs were a band, what kind of music would they sing?
The blues.

If two's company and three's a crowd, what are four and five?
Nine.

Would you look at my car and tell me if my blinkers are working?
Yes, no, yes, no, yes, no.

That's a strange pair of socks you're wearing. One is green and the other is blue with polka dots.
That's not so strange. I have another pair just like it at home.

❖ ❖ ❖

"Is this boat tilting, or is it my imagination?" Tom asked listlessly.

16

Who's There?

Knock, knock.
Who's there?
Cereal.
Cereal who?
Cereal (see you real) soon.

Knock, knock.
Who's there?
Pasta.
Pasta who?
Pasta (pass the) pizza under the door—I'm
  starved.

Knock, knock.
Who's there?
Pizza.
Pizza who?
Pizza (Pete's a) nice guy.

Knock, knock.
Who's there?
B.C.
B.C. who?
B.C.-ing you!

Knock, knock.
Who's there?
Ida.
Ida who?
I'd appreciate it if you'd open the door.

Knock, knock.
Who's there?
Ya!
Ya who?
I'm glad you are having fun.

Knock, knock.
Who's there?
Anita.
Anita who?
Anita take a bath.

Knock, knock.
Who's there?
Dogs.
Dogs who?
No they don't—owls who. Dogs bark.

17

Believe It or Not!

What causes those giant circular ocean
  currents called gyres?
Earth's rotation.

Who was Spain's first bullfighter?
El Cid in A.D. 1040.

How much air will you breathe in a lifetime?
Enough to fill 2½ large blimps.

What does one square inch of skin contain?
*An average of 645 sweat glands, 63 hairs, 18
  feet of blood vessels, and 78 yards of nerves.*

What happens to a baby giraffe when it's
    born?
*It drops six feet to the ground and lands on its
    head.*

Who wrote the famous songs "God Bless
    America" and "White Christmas"?
Irving Berlin.

How big are the largest stars in the universe?
About 100 times bigger than our sun.

How many countries in the world have no
    coastline?
37.

What is the town in Montana with the
    smallest population?
Vergelle—population three.

What color is the milk of a yak?
Pink.

What birds hold funerals for their dead?
*Magpies. When one dies, the others
  ceremoniously fly over and each in turn
  swoops to peck once at the dead bird.*

What country has the most donut shops per
  capita?
Canada.

What is the most popular piano tune ever
  written and who wrote it?
"Chopsticks," written by Arthur de Lulli.

Do some mushrooms eat bird feathers?
Yes.

Is a buffalo born with its hump?
*No, that comes with age. A buffalo calf looks
  pretty much like any reddish brown
  barnyard calf.*

Do whale songs rhyme?
Yes.

How can gulls drink seawater safely?
They have glands in their heads to desalinate it.

When was toilet paper invented?
In 1857 by Joseph C. Gayetty of New York City.

What's the most popular ornamental plant in the world?
The rose.

How tall is a newly hatched ostrich chick?
A foot or so. Then it grows about a foot a month.

According to experts, how long should a bed be?
It should be ten inches longer than the sleeper.

What is a gephyrophobic?
*Someone who is afraid of crossing bridges
    over water.*

Who was the first American to win a Nobel
    Peace Prize?
Teddy Roosevelt.

Who invented the graham cracker?
Sylvester Graham.

Where can you find a scrub fowl bird?
*On the island of Melville off the coast of
    Australia.*

Can you lead a cow upstairs or downstairs?
Only upstairs.

18

Percival & Lacy

Percival: What never asks questions, but is
  often answered?
Lacy: I have no clue.
Percival: A doorbell.

Percival: What does Forrest Gump say on
  Valentine's Day?
Lacy: I don't know.
Percival: Cupid is as Cupid does.

Percival: What animals are well educated?
Lacy: I can't guess.
Percival: Fish, because they go around in
  schools.

Percival: What kind of gum do bees chew?
Lacy: I have no idea.
Percival: Bumble gum.

Percival: What do you call a banana that gets run over by an eighteen wheeler?
Lacy: You tell me.
Percival: Banana splat.

Percival: What do cheerleaders drink for lunch?
Lacy: I give up.
Percival: Root beer.

Percival: What cake do baseball players like best?
Lacy: Who knows?
Percival: A bunt cake.

Percival: What is a sound sleeper?
Lacy: You've got me.
Percival: Someone who snores.

Percival: What color would you paint the sun and the wind?

Lacy: My mind is a blank.

Percival: The sun "rose" and the wind "blue."

Percival: What do snakes do after they have a fight?

Lacy: That's a mystery.

Percival: They hiss and make up.

Percival: What is black, white, and green all over?

Lacy: I'm blank.

Percival: A seasick skunk.

Percival: What kind of car do cows drive?

Lacy: I don't have the foggiest.

Percival: "Cattle" cars.

Percival: What did the mountain say to the earthquake?

Lacy: I give up.

Percival: It's not my fault.

Percival: What is a volcano?
Lacy: It's unknown to me.
Percival: A mountain with the hiccups.

Percival: What is drawn by everyone without
pen or pencil?
Lacy: I'm in the dark.
Percival: Breath.

19

Moe & Clem

Moe: What do you call a dinosaur from south
of the border?
Clem: I have no clue.
Moe: Tyrannosaurus Mex.

Moe: What do mangos like to read?
Clem: I don't know.
Moe: A mango-zine.

Moe: What kind of furniture likes pop music?
Clem: I can't guess.
Moe: A rocking chair.

Moe: What is a carton of milk's favorite game?
Clem: I have no idea.
Moe: Follow the liter.

Moe: What side of a chicken has the most feathers?
Clem: You tell me.
Moe: The outside.

Moe: What is a lumberjack's favorite month?
Clem: I give up.
Moe: Septimber.

Moe: What is brown and has a head and a tail but no legs?
Clem: Who knows?
Moe: A penny.

Moe: What are goosebumps for?
Clem: You've got me.
Moe: To keep the geese from speeding.

Moe: What's holding up Bugs Bunny's latest movie?
Clem: My mind is a blank.
Moe: Carrot negotiations.

Moe: What did the momma door say to the baby door?
Clem: That's a mystery.
Moe: You're a-door-able!

Moe: What has four heads and no body?
Clem: I'm blank.
Moe: Mount Rushmore.

Moe: What do gingerbread boys put on their beds?
Clem: I don't have the foggiest.
Moe: Cookie sheets.

Moe: What has a red suit, a big bag, and falls down chimneys?
Clem: I give up.
Moe: Santa Klutz.

Moe: What's a slinky's favorite season?
Clem: It's unknown to me.
Moe: Spring.

Moe: What do you call flowers that are really
    good friends?
Clem: I'm in the dark.
Moe: Best buds.

Moe: What did the little frog say to the big
    frog?
Clem: Search me.
Moe: One more game of leap frog and I'll
    croak.

20

Something to Think About!

What would cause the oceans of the world to rise by three feet?
A rise in temperature of two degrees.

What country once used engraved bamboo as legal money?
China.

What is the most significant innovation of all time in the cosmetics industry?
The safety razor.

Where is the largest portrait head in the world found?
Mount Rushmore.

The world's largest ranch is in what country?
Canada.

Why are Maine lobsters so prized?
Colder water lets them mature more slowly, so they have time to get bigger.

How much milk can a mother whale produce?
200 quarts in 24 hours.

How fast can a chicken travel?
Up to nine miles per hour.

What time of year are the most batteries sold?
During the 30 days before Christmas.

Which has the most species—horseflies or
  horses?
Horseflies.

Are Turkish towels from Turkey?
No, they are French.

How much pizza do Americans eat each day?
7.5 acres.

How many dreams per year does the average
  person have?
1,460.

How many terms did President Washington
  serve?
Two.

What is the smallest known shark?
The cigar shark, which is 4½ inches long.

"Offside," "hooking," and "boarding" are all
rule violations for what sport?
Hockey.

A certain sea creature walks on the tips of its
teeth. Which is it?
The sea urchin.

Name the oldest science—the study of stars
and planets.
Astronomy.

Can gorillas swim?
No.

Horses can sleep standing up—true or false?
True.

The world's smallest continent is one large
country. Name it.
Australia.

How old was Mary Stuart when she became
  Queen of Scots—one week old, ten years
  old, or 17 years old?
One week.

What Danish author wrote such classics as
  "The Red Shoes," "The Ugly Duckling," and
  "The Snow Queen"?
Hans Christian Andersen.

If you calculate by strength to relative weight,
  which is stronger—an elephant or a bumble
  bee?
*A bumble bee is 150 times stronger than an
  elephant.*

What canal separates Africa from Asia?
The Suez Canal.

What swimming stroke has the name of an
  insect?
The butterfly.

21

Scrambled Words

(Answers on page 91)

Here's a scramble with letters to sort. The right answer is a type of sport.
tkrca nda lefid

Here's a scramble with letters to sort. The right answer is a type of sport.
tnotrihla

Word scramble with letters to sort. The right answer is a type of sport.
xbgion

Can you figure out this scramble with letters to sort. The right answer is a type of sport.

gtewih ftglini

Here's a scramble you can tame. The right answer is a type of game.

akcobmnagm

Here's a scramble with letters to sort. The right answer is a type of sport.

sheohsroes

Word scramble with letters to sort. The right answer is a type of sport.

ismwgnim

Can you figure out this scramble with letters to sort? The right answer is a type of sport.

rehacyr

Here's a scramble with letters to sort. The right answer is a type of sport.

sorcs-rynutco nsikig

22

Kati & Zelda

Kati: Why did the zebra cross the road?
Zelda: I have no clue.
Kati: To prove that it was not a chicken.

Kati: Why did the young man go into the
pizza business?
Zelda: I don't know.
Kati: He wanted to make some dough.

Kati: Why is this bread full of holes?
Zelda: I can't guess.
Kati: It's hole wheat bread.

Kati: Why shouldn't you tell these jokes to
your friends while ice-skating?
Zelda: I have no idea.
Kati: The ice might crack up!

Kati: Why do dogs bury bones in the ground?
Zelda: You tell me.
Kati: Because you can't bury them in the sky!

Kati: Why did the rooster crow before
daybreak?
Zelda: I give up.
Kati: His cluck was fast!

Kati: Why do elephants wear sandals?
Zelda: Who knows?
Kati: To stop their feet from sinking into the
sand.

Kati: Why is it so hard to drive a nail?
Zelda: You've got me.
Kati: Because it doesn't have a steering
wheel.

94

Kati: Why does a baseball pitcher raise one leg when he pitches?

Zelda: My mind is a blank.

Kati: If he raised both legs, he would fall down.

Kati: Why does it get hot after a basketball game?

Zelda: That's a mystery.

Kati: Because all the fans have gone.

Kati: Why does it take longer to run from second base to third base than it takes to run from first base to second base?

Zelda: I'm blank.

Kati: Because there's a shortstop between second and third.

Kati: Why was the basketball player holding his nose?

Zelda: I don't have the foggiest.

Kati: Someone was taking a foul shot.

Kati: Why did the football coach send in his second string?
Zelda: I give up.
Kati: To tie up the game.

Kati: Why do elephants have wrinkled legs?
Zelda: It's unknown to me.
Kati: Because they tie their tennis shoes too tight.

Kati: Why was George Washington buried standing up?
Zelda: I'm in the dark.
Kati: Because he never lied.

Kati: Why did the cowboy aim his gun at the fan?
Zelda: Search me.
Kati: He was just shooting the breeze.

23

Myrtle & Maynard

Myrtle: What do you get when you go to sleep
with cookies in your bed?
Maynard: I have no clue.
Myrtle: A crummy night sleep.

Myrtle: What's worse then finding a worm in
your apple?
Maynard: I don't know.
Myrtle: Finding half a worm.

Myrtle: What musical toy plays sports?
Maynard: I can't guess.
Myrtle: Jock-in-the-box.

Myrtle: What kind of milk do you get from a cow in Alaska?

Maynard: I have no idea.

Myrtle: Cold cream.

Myrtle: What do you call a cow whose calf has been taken from her?

Maynard: You tell me.

Myrtle: Decaffeinated.

Myrtle: What is bought by the yard and worn by the foot?

Maynard: I give up.

Myrtle: A carpet.

Myrtle: What is the world's greatest milkshake?

Maynard: Who knows?

Myrtle: A cow on a trampoline.

Myrtle: What is the hardest thing about riding a bull?
Maynard: You've got me.
Myrtle: The ground.

Myrtle: What is a mosquito's favorite sport?
Maynard: My mind is a blank.
Myrtle: Skin diving.

Myrtle: What day do fish hate most?
Maynard: That's a mystery.
Myrtle: Fryday (Friday).

Myrtle: What kind of magazine do dogs hate?
Maynard: I'm blank.
Myrtle: A cat-alog.

Myrtle: What do we know about the insides of a cherry?
Maynard: I don't have the foggiest.
Myrtle: They're the pits!

Myrtle: What vegetable is essential to good
    music?
Maynard: I give up.
Myrtle: The beet.

Myrtle: What goes around your head and
    plays music?
Maynard: It's unknown to me.
Myrtle: A headband.

24

For Your Information

The first agency of the United States
government was Indian Affairs. What was
the second?
United States Post Office.

How deep would the water covering the earth
be if the earth's surface were perfectly
smooth?
About a mile and a half.

What are cackle berries?
Hens' eggs.

How fast do shifting continents move?
As fast as fingernails grow.

Did Alexander the Great ever lose a military
 battle?
*Not one. Neither did the Duke of Wellington or
 Julius Caesar.*

What are the two times that perfume sales
 are the greatest?
*During war and during an economic
 depression.*

What is the literal definition of mortgage?
"Death pledge."

What city gets the most rain per year?
Monrovia, in Liberia, gets 202 inches per year.

How often do bats hibernate?
*Every time they go to sleep. Whenever they
 doze off, their body temperatures drop to
 that of the surrounding air.*

How many country music radio stations are
   there in the United States?
More than 2,000.

How thick is the average spinal cord?
One-half inch thick.

If you are lost in the woods and starving,
   what item of clothing should you eat?
*Your shoes—leather has some nutritional
   value.*

What sport was once illegal in many states?
Bowling—it was illegal in the mid-1840s.

Which has the smaller antennae—a butterfly
   or a moth?
*A butterfly. They have thinner antennae with
   little knobs on the ends.*

All the people featured on coins face left
except one. Who is the president who faces
right?
Abraham Lincoln, on the penny.

How does an orangutan tell you to stay out of
its territory?
It lets out a raging burp.

What is a polecat?
A weasel.

How much do baby robins eat?
14 feet of earthworms every day.

What word was once considered a dirty word
in England?
"Pants," in the 1880s.

What kind of pillows did the ancient
Egyptians sleep on?
Pillows made of stone.

How many times each year do your eyes
  blink?
About 84,000,000 times.

What do your fingers and your tongue have in
  common?
They all have a print that is different.

25

Dork & Mork

Dork: What can you put in a glass but never take out of it?
Mork: I have no clue.
Dork: A crack.

Dork: What store do dogs hate?
Mork: I don't know.
Dork: The flea market.

Dork: What do you call a retired postman?
Mork: I have no idea.
Dork: A man who has no zip.

Dork: What do you get when you cross a pig and a porcupine?

Mork: You tell me.

Dork: A pork-upine.

Dork: What did the VCR say to the CD player?

Mork: I give up.

Dork: You just don't get the picture, do you?

Dork: What's the best way to catch a chicken?

Mork: Who knows?

Dork: Hide in the coop and make a noise like a bread crumb!

Dork: What was my name two days ago?

Mork: Dork.

Dork: What was my name yesterday?

Mork: Dork.

Dork: Knock, knock.

Mork: Who's there?

Dork: See? You've forgotten me already.

Dork: What did they award to the man who
   invented door knockers?
Mork: My mind is a blank.
Dork: The no-bell prize.

Dork: What goes tick-tock-woof?
Mork: That's a mystery.
Dork: A watchdog.

Dork: What do you get if you tie two bikes
   together?
Mork: I'm blank.
Dork: Siamese Schwinns.

Dork: What do you call a radical chicken?
Mork: I don't have the foggiest.
Dork: A left-winger!

Dork: What do they call a chicken who keeps
   missing free throws in a basketball game?
Mork: I give up
Dork: A fowl up!

Dork: What's another expression for chicken
feed?
Mork: It's unknown to me.
Dork: A poultry sum!

Dork: What goes "clip"?
Mork: I'm in the dark.
Dork: A one-legged horse.

26

Side Splitters

Two birds were flying as a jet crossed by. "Did you see how fast that bird was flying?" asked one bird. The other bird replied, "You would fly like that, too, if your backside was on fire."

Referee: Now remember, at the bell, shake hands.
Boxer: I don't have to remember. Mine are shaking already.

Deputy: I hear that a charging rhino won't hurt you if you carry a flashlight.
Sheriff: True—if you carry it fast enough.

Georgie: I wish I had the money to buy a
million basketballs.
Porgie: What would you do with a million
basketballs?
Georgie: Nothing. I just want the money.

Shopper in sports shop: May I have a baseball
glove for my son?
Clerk: Sorry, madam, we don't swap.

First Robot: Do you have any brothers?
Second Robot: No, only transistors.

Traveler: I'd like a round-trip ticket for a
train ride to Seattle.
Ticket Seller: I'm sorry—all our tickets are
square.

Georgie: Have you ever seen a line drive?
Porgie: No, but I've seen a ball park.

Glenda: I had shoes stolen from under my
nose last night.
Brenda: That's a funny place to wear them.

Game Warden: Have you ever hunted bear?
Tourist: No, but I've gone water skiing in my
shorts.

Farmer: Do you realize it takes three sheep to
make one sweater?
City Man: Amazing—I didn't even know they
could knit.

Jeckle: I'm going on a safari to Africa.
Heckle: Drop us a lion.

Tip: I was down at the lake and I saw a
catfish.
Top: Really? How did it hold the rod?

Falling in love is like a sweet dream.
Getting married is like an alarm clock.

27

Winifred & Thaddaeus

Winifred: What do you get when you cross a giraffe, a glass, and a cow?
Thaddaeus: I have no clue.
Winifred: A tall glass of milk.

Winifred: What food is good for your eyes?
Thaddaeus: I don't know.
Winifred: Seafood.

Winifred: What did the doctor say to the banana?
Thaddaeus: I can't guess.
Winifred: Are you peeling all right?

Winifred: What dog is always quiet?
Thaddaeus: I have no idea.
Winifred: A hush puppy.

Winifred: What did one eye say to the other eye?
Thaddaeus: You tell me.
Winifred: Between you and me, something smells!

Winifred: What is the favorite color of reptiles?
Thaddaeus: I give up.
Winifred: Green.

Winifred: What do you call a really scared tree?
Thaddaeus: Who knows?
Winifred: Petrified.

Winifred: What do pigs do when they play basketball?
Thaddaeus: You've got me.
Winifred: Hog the ball.

❖ ❖ ❖

Winifred: What did the policeman say to the three angels?
Thaddaeus: That's a mystery.
Winifred: Halo, halo, halo.

Winifred: What do you call a cat who has just swallowed a duck?
Thaddaeus: I'm blank.
Winifred: A duck-filled fatty puss.

Winifred: What color is a marriage?
Thaddaeus: I don't have the foggiest.
Winifred: Wed.

28

More Fantastic Thoughts

What insect recycles?
Spiders build new webs daily after they tear down and eat the previous day's web.

The first badminton birdie ever used was made from a champagne cork stuck with feathers.

Willie Shoemaker is the most famous _____ in the world. Lightweight champion, Olympic gymnast, or American jockey?
American jockey.

Samuel L. Clemens was the real name of
what famous writer?
Mark Twain.

In what sport might you find a birdie and an
eagle?
Golf.

Why do cans of diet cola float while cans of
regular colas sink?
*Sugar and corn syrup weigh more than
artificial sweeteners.*

What do you call a person who leads an
orchestra?
Conductor.

The largest planet in our solar system is more
than 1,300 times the size of Earth. Which
is it?
Jupiter.

True or false—when you sneeze air travels
out of your lungs at about 100 miles per
hour.

True.

How many hearts do eels have?

Two.

When were right and left shoes first made?

*In 1818. Before that, both shoes in a pair were
identical.*

How many insects are there on one square
mile of rural land?

*More than there are human beings on the
entire earth.*

What Jello flavors were flops?

*Apple, cola, celery, salad, and mixed
vegetable.*

How much liquid does your largest salivary
   gland secrete in your lifetime?
*About 25,000 quarts—enough to fill 125
   bathtubs.*

What is more nutritious than a pound of
   beef?
*A pound of grasshoppers is three times more
   nutritious than beef.*

   The shortest baseball game recorded was
52 minutes long. It was played between the
New York Giants and the Philadelphia
Phillies in 1919.

Why do sharks have to swim constantly?
*Because they have no air bladders, so they
   must swim or they sink.*

A football player enters what area of the field
   to score a touchdown?
The end zone.

What are the ancient, elaborate tombs in
   Egypt called?
Pyramids.

On what island did Napoleon make his home?
   (He also died there.)
St. Helena.

What killed off the dodo bird?
Pigs.

What is the legal name for the Popsicle?
Frozen confection.

What is a sea wasp?
A jelly fish.

Which grows faster—fingernails or toenails?
Fingernails grow four times faster.

Where is it illegal to tie a giraffe to a
   telephone pole?
Atlanta, Georgia.

29

Reginald & Bartholomew

Reginald: What is a mouse's favorite dessert?
Bartholomew: I have no clue.
Reginald: Cheesecake.

Reginald: What do you call a person who
steals soap?
Bartholomew: I don't know.
Reginald: A dirty crook.

Reginald: What did one knife say to the other
knife?
Bartholomew: I can't guess.
Reginald: You're looking mighty sharp.

Reginald: What did one chicken say to its mother before going to bed?

Bartholomew: I have no idea.

Reginald: I'm egg-zhausted!

Reginald: What do you call a car you can only drive in the fall?

Bartholomew: You tell me.

Reginald: An autumn-mobile.

Reginald: What food will never become heavyweight champion of the world?

Bartholomew: I give up.

Reginald: The lollipop—because it's always getting licked.

Reginald: What do police officers put on their peanut butter sandwiches?

Bartholomew: Who knows?

Reginald: Traffic jam.

Reginald: What color is rain?
Bartholomew: You've got me.
Reginald: Water color.

Reginald: What did King Kong say when his sister had a baby?
Bartholomew: My mind is a blank.
Reginald: Well, I'll be a monkey's uncle.

Reginald: What did the baby corn say to his mother?
Bartholomew: That's a mystery.
Reginald: Where's pop-corn?

Reginald: What do you get when you cross a chicken and a hog?
Bartholomew: I'm blank.
Reginald: A hog-boiled egg.

Reginald: What do a tree and a dog have in common?
Bartholomew: I don't have the foggiest.
Reginald: They both have a bark.

Reginald: What newspaper did the cave men
  read?
Bartholomew: I give up
Reginald: *The Prehistoric Times.*

Reginald: What do you call a sheared sheep?
Bartholomew: It's unknown to me.
Reginald: A bare, bare, back sheep.

30

Tami & Twila

Tami: Why was the chicken scared to cross
the road?
Twila: I have no clue.
Tami: Because Colonel Sanders was on the
other side.

Tami: Why did God give us toes?
Twila: I don't know.
Tami: To find furniture in the middle of the
night.

Tami: Why does the ballerina wear a tutu?
Twila: I can't guess.
Tami: Because the one-one's too small and the
three-three's too big.

Tami: Why are flowers so lazy?

Twila: I have no idea.

Tami: Because you'll always find them in
  beds.

Tami: Why did the firecracker go to the
  barbershop?

Twila: You tell me.

Tami: To get its "bangs" cut.

Tami: Why did Santa have only eight reindeer
  on Christmas Eve?

Twila: I give up.

Tami: Because Comet was home cleaning the
  kitchen.

Tami: Why are movie stars cool?

Twila: Who knows?

Tami: Because they have so many fans.

Tami: Why do cows chew their cud?
Twila: You've got me.
Tami: They don't have money for gum.

Tami: Why did the scientist quit her job studying mummies?
Twila: My mind is a blank.
Tami: She was too wrapped up in her work.

Tami: Why did the banana go out with the plum?
Twila: That's a mystery.
Tami: Because he couldn't get a date.

Tami: Why did the farmer feed his cows money?
Twila: I'm blank.
Tami: He wanted rich milk.

Tami: Why is it so easy to weigh a fish?
Twila: I don't have the foggiest.
Tami: Because they come with their own scales.

Tami: Why did Dino chase the bunny out of his duck pond?
Twila: I give up.
Tami: He didn't want hare on his "quackers."

Tami: Why do people wear sunglasses?
Twila: It's unknown to me.
Tami: Because moon glasses are too dark.

Tami: Why does Father Time wear bandages?
Twila: I'm in the dark.
Tami: Because day breaks and night falls.

Tami: Why did the man hold up a slice of bread?
Twila: Search me.
Tami: To propose a toast.

31

Doctor / Doctor

Doctor: How is the boy who swallowed a
   dollar bill?
Nurse: There's no change yet.

Patient: Doctor, I swallowed a chicken bone!
Doctor: Are you choking?
Patient: No, I'm serious!

Patient: Doctor, doctor, a crate of eggs fell on
   my head!
Doctor: Well, the yolk's on you!

Doctor: Strange . . . Your brother is very small compared to you.

Patient: Sure, he's my half-brother.

Patient: Doctor, doctor, my eyesight is getting worse!

Doctor: You're absolutely right. This is a post office.

Doctor: Mr. Johnson, I think you're suffering from a split personality.

Mr. Johnson: No, we're not.

Patient: Doctor, doctor, my stomach hurts!

Doctor: Stop bellyaching!

Doctor: Do you sleep on your left side or your right side?

Patient: I sleep on both sides. All of me goes to sleep at once.

Patient: Doctor, the first 30 minutes that I'm up every morning, I feel dizzy. What should I do?
Doctor: Get up half an hour later.

Doctor: Does your family suffer from insanity?
Patient: No, we kind of enjoy it.

32

Dottie & Ignatius

Dottie: What do you call an elephant without any ears?
Ignatius: I have no clue.
Dottie: Whatever you want; it can't hear you.

Dottie: What should a fullback do when he gets a handoff?
Ignatius: I don't know.
Dottie: Go to a secondhand store.

Dottie: What's black and white and sticky all over?
Ignatius: I can't guess.
Dottie: A referee who fell into the Sugar Bowl.

❖ ❖ ❖

Dottie: What disease makes you a better
 basketball player?
Ignatius: I have no idea.
Dottie: Athlete's foot.

❖ ❖ ❖

Dottie: What is a cheerleader's favorite color?
Ignatius: You tell me.
Dottie: Yeller.

❖ ❖ ❖

Dottie: What would you do if you found a sick
 bird?
Ignatius: I give up.
Dottie: Give it first aid tweetment.

❖ ❖ ❖

Dottie: What is the first letter in yellow?
Ignatius: "Y."
Dottie: Because I want to know.

❖ ❖ ❖

Dottie: What is a hermit?
Ignatius: You've got me.
Dottie: A girl's baseball glove.

❖ ❖ ❖

Dottie: What is the best way to count cows?
Ignatius: My mind is a blank.
Dottie: With a cow-culator.

Dottie: What's the difference between a
   Martian and a snoo?
Ignatius: What's a snoo?
Dottie: Nothing much. What's snoo with you?

Dottie: What happened when the horse
   swallowed a dollar?
Ignatius: I'm blank.
Dottie: It bucked.

Dottie: What kind of fur do you get from a
   wild tiger?
Ignatius: I don't have the foggiest.
Dottie: As fur as you can get.

Dottie: What does my mother do for a
   headache?
Ignatius: I give up.
Dottie: She sends my brother and me out to
   play.

33

Question & Answer

Who was the first man in space?
The man in the moon.

❖ ❖ ❖

Where does the funniest president live?
In the Wit House.

❖ ❖ ❖

Did you hear the watermelon joke?
It's pitiful.

❖ ❖ ❖

In 1620, why did the Pilgrims set sail on the
Mayflower?
Because the Aprilflower had already left.

Who robbed stagecoaches and wore dirty
    clothes?
Messy James.

How do you mend a broken jack-o-lantern?
With a pumpkin patch.

In what kind of home does the buffalo roam?
A very dirty one.

Whose fault will it be if California falls into
    the ocean?
San Andreas' fault.

How do you hold a bat?
By the wings.

If dogs have fleas, what do sheep have?
Fleece.

When can you jump while sitting down?
While playing checkers.

Is chicken soup good for your health?
Not if you're a chicken.

How can you make a fly ball?
Hit him with a bat.

On what day do you moan the most?
On Moan-day.

When is an umpire like a telephone operator?
When he makes a call.

How do you make a hot dog roll?
Tilt your plate.

34

Filbert & Freeda

Filbert: What happened when the driver
leaped 100 feet into a glass of cola?
Freeda: I have no clue.
Filbert: Nothing. It was a soft drink.

Filbert: What is green and dangerous?
Freeda: I don't know.
Filbert: A thundering herd of pickles.

Filbert: What do you call a joking duck?
Freeda: I can't guess.
Filbert: A wise-quacker.

Filbert: What would you call a short,
sunburned outlaw riding a horse?
Freeda: I have no idea.
Filbert: Little Red Riding Hood.

Filbert: What would you get if you crossed
Billy the Kid and a cow?
Freeda: You tell me.
Filbert: Better not try it. Billy the Kid doesn't
like to be crossed.

Filbert: What does a rabbit say when
someone knocks on the door?
Freeda: I give up.
Filbert: Some "bunny" get that.

Filbert: What kind of thief steals cats?
Freeda: You've got me.
Filbert: A purr-snatcher.

Filbert: What was the farmer doing on the
other side of the road?
Freeda: My mind is a blank.
Filbert: Catching all the chickens who tried to
cross the road.

Filbert: What happens when baseball players get old?

Freeda: I have no clue.

Filbert: They go batty.

Filbert: What do you do with a green hockey player?

Freeda: I don't know.

Filbert: Wait until he ripens.

Filbert: What gets harder to catch the faster you run?

Freeda: I can't guess.

Filbert: Your breath.

Filbert: What kind of animal eats and drinks with its tail?

Freeda: I have no idea.

Filbert: They all do. No animal takes off its tail to eat or drink.

Filbert: What did the ocean say to the beach?
Freeda: I'm blank.
Filbert: I'm not shore.

Filbert: What lives in the water and takes
you anywhere you want to go?
Freeda: You tell me.
Filbert: A taxi crab.

35

Bartholomew & Bertha

Bartholomew: How does the ocean say
  good-bye?
Bertha: I have no clue.
Bartholomew: I'll be sea-ing you!

Bartholomew: Where do frogs shop?
Bertha: I don't know.
Bartholomew: Montgomery Wart.

Bartholomew: How do you say good-bye to the
  ocean?
Bertha: I can't guess.
Bartholomew: With a wave.

Bartholomew: Which animal loves dumb jokes the most?

Bertha: I have no idea.

Bartholomew: A punda bear.

Bartholomew: How do hangmen keep up with current events?

Bertha: I'm blank.

Bartholomew: They read the noose-paper.

Bartholomew: Who was the thirstiest outlaw in the West?

Bertha: You tell me.

Bartholomew: The one who drank Canada Dry.

Bartholomew: How did the midget qualify for the basketball team?

Bertha: I give up.

Bartholomew: He lied about his height.

Bartholomew: Where did the Pilgrims hang their hats?

Bertha: You've got me.

Bartholomew: On Plymouth Rack.

Bartholomew: How do cowboys drive steers?

Bertha: My mind is a blank.

Bartholomew: With steer-ing wheels.

Bartholomew: Where do calves eat?

Bertha: I don't have the foggiest.

Bartholomew: In calf-eterias.

Bartholomew: How do you ship baby horses?

Bertha: I have no clue.

Bartholomew: By Pony Express.

Bartholomew: Who was the most famous cat in the Wild West?

Bertha: I don't know.

Bartholomew: Kit-ty Carson.

Bartholomew: How much do you have to
know to teach a cat tricks?
Bertha: I can't guess.
Bartholomew: More than the cat.

Bartholomew: Which national monument
honors poison ivy?
Bertha: I have no idea.
Bartholomew: Mount Rashmore.

Bartholomew: How do you make a horse
float?
Bertha: I'm blank.
Bartholomew: Take two scoops of ice cream,
root beer—and add one horse.

36

Igor & Theda

Igor: What do you do to a bad ping-pong ball?
Theda: I have no clue.
Igor: Paddle it.

Igor: What does a male sheep do when he gets angry?
Theda: I don't know.
Igor: He goes on a ram-page.

Igor: What was Ronald McDonald's medical problem?
Theda: I can't guess.
Igor: Fallen arches.

Igor: What position do pigs play on a baseball team?
Theda: I have no idea.
Igor: Short-slop.

Igor: What do you call a deer with no eyes?
Theda: I'm blank.
Igor: No-eye-deer (no idea).

Igor: What was a spider doing on the baseball team?
Theda: You tell me.
Igor: Catching flies.

Igor: What happens when you hit a pop fly?
Theda: I give up.
Igor: The same thing that happens when you hit a mom fly—the whole fly family gets mad.

Igor: What does a skunk do when it disagrees with the umpire?
Theda: You've got me.
Igor: It raises a stink.

Igor: What would you get if you crossed a
lobster and a baseball player?
Theda: My mind is a blank.
Igor: A pinch hitter.

Igor: What do you get if you cover a baseball
field with sandpaper?
Theda: I don't have the foggiest.
Igor: A diamond in the rough.

Igor: What did the scientist get when she
crossed an electric eel and a sponge?
Theda: I have no clue.
Igor: Shock absorbers.

Igor: What snacks should you serve
mechanics at parties?
Theda: I don't know.
Igor: Assorted nuts and bolts.

Igor: What would you get if you crossed a
porcupine and an alarm clock?
Theda: I can't guess.
Igor: A stickler for punctuality.

Igor: What would you get if you crossed a
   parrot and an elephant?
Theda: I have no idea.
Igor: Something that tells everything it
   remembers.

37

Delbert & Darlene

Delbert: Why did the chicken cross the basketball court?
Darlene: I have no clue.
Delbert: Because the referee called a fowl.

Delbert: Why were outlaws the strongest men in the Old West?
Darlene: I don't know.
Delbert: They could hold up trains.

Delbert: Why did the goose cross the road?
Darlene: I can't guess.
Delbert: Because the light was green.

Delbert: Why did the policeman go to the
  barbecue?
Darlene: I have no idea.
Delbert: He heard it was a place to have a
  steak out.

Delbert: Why are there bridges over water?
Darlene: I'm blank.
Delbert: So people won't step on the fishes.

Delbert: Why don't most donkeys go to
  college?
Darlene: You tell me.
Delbert: Because not many graduate from
  high school.

Delbert: Why did the mother owl take her
  baby to the doctor?
Darlene: I give up.
Delbert: Because it didn't give a hoot.

Delbert: Why couldn't Robin play baseball?
Darlene: You've got me.
Delbert: He forgot his bat, man.

Delbert: Why did the turtle cross the road?
Darlene: My mind is a blank.
Delbert: To get to the Shell station.

Delbert: Why did the otter cross the road?
Darlene: I don't have the foggiest.
Delbert: To get to the otter side.

Delbert: Why did the scientist study
electricity?
Darlene: I have no clue.
Delbert: He wanted to keep up with current
events.

Delbert: Why can't you play hide-and-seek
with baby chickens?
Darlene: I don't know.
Delbert: Because they're always peeping.

38

Abigail & Argyle

Abigail: What rolls into a ball whenever there's a fire?
Argyle: I have no clue.
Abigail: An alarmadillo.

Abigail: What do baby sweet potatoes sleep in?
Argyle: I don't know.
Abigail: Their yammies.

Abigail: What do you call someone who raises skunks?
Argyle: I can't guess.
Abigail: The farmer in the smell.

❖ ❖ ❖

Abigail: What would you get if you crossed a
rabbit and a frog?
Argyle: I have no idea.
Abigail: A bunny ribbit.

❖ ❖ ❖

Abigail: What makes the road broad?
Argyle: I'm blank.
Abigail: The letter "b."

❖ ❖ ❖

Abigail: What do you say when you meet a
toad?
Argyle: You tell me.
Abigail: Wart's new?

❖ ❖ ❖

Abigail: What's a cow's favorite TV show?
Argyle: I give up.
Abigail: *Steer Trek.*

❖ ❖ ❖

Abigail: What is a bee's favorite song?
Argyle: You've got me.
Abigail: "Stinging in the Rain."

❖ ❖ ❖

Abigail: What lives in a river, lies in the mud, and grows antlers?
Argyle: My mind is a blank.
Abigail: A hippopotamoose.

Abigail: What did the father buffalo say to his son when he went off to school?
Argyle: I don't have the foggiest.
Abigail: Bison!

Abigail: What is soft, white, and comes from Mars?
Argyle: I have no clue.
Abigail: Martian-mallows.

Abigail: What's the pigs' favorite TV show?
Argyle: I don't know.
Abigail: *Ham Improvement.*

Abigail: What do astronauts do when they get dirty?
Argyle: I can't guess.
Abigail: They take a meteor shower.

Abigail: What do you call a slow American?
Argyle: I have no idea.
Abigail: A Yankee Dawdle.

Abigail: What home computers grow on trees?
Argyle: I'm blank.
Abigail: Apples.

Abigail: What do you call a horse that likes
arts and crafts?
Argyle: You tell me.
Abigail: A hobby horse.

39

Egor & Edith

Egor: Why do cows live in barns?
Edith: I have no clue.
Egor: They're too big for birdhouses.

Egor: Why did the weatherman let a grizzly
  sit on him?
Edith: I don't know.
Egor: He wanted to measure the bearometric
  pressure.

Egor: Why did the rabbit cross the road?
Edith: I can't guess.
Egor: To get to the hopping mall.

Egor: Why did the female horse enter the city
   election?
Edith: I have no idea.
Egor: She wanted to run for mare.

Egor: Why is it dangerous to play cards in the
   jungle?
Edith: I'm blank.
Egor: Because of all the cheetahs.

Egor: Why did the politician wear jogging
   shorts?
Edith: You tell me.
Egor: He wanted to run for office.

Egor: Why did the dinosaur cross the road?
Edith: I give up.
Egor: Because in those days they didn't have
   chickens.

Egor: Why did the cow cross the road?
Edith: My mind is a blank.
Egor: To see its fodder.

Egor: Why did the lady leave her
  handkerchief under the tree?
Edith: I don't have the foggiest.
Egor: Because it was a weeping willow.

Egor: Why did the teacher wear loud socks?
Edith: I have no clue.
Egor: So his feet wouldn't fall asleep.

Egor: Why did the banana leave the movie?
Edith: I don't know.
Egor: It didn't appeal to him.

Egor: Why do they say bowling is good for
  teenagers?
Edith: I can't guess.
Egor: Because it takes them off the streets
  and puts them in the alleys.

40

Mortimer & Matilda

Mortimer: What do you call a mountain climber who is afraid of heights?
Matilda: I have no clue.
Mortimer: A failure.

Mortimer: What did the girl sea say when the boy sea asked her for a date?
Matilda: I don't know.
Mortimer: Shore.

Mortimer: What is brown and white and turns cartwheels?
Matilda: I can't guess.
Mortimer: A brown and white horse pulling a cart.

❖ ❖ ❖

Mortimer: What could you call the small rivers that flow into the Nile?

Matilda: I have no idea.

Mortimer: Juveniles.

❖ ❖ ❖

Mortimer: What season is it when you're on a trampoline?

Matilda: I'm blank.

Mortimer: Springtime.

❖ ❖ ❖

Mortimer: What did the gum say to the trashcan?

Matilda: You tell me.

Mortimer: I'll stick with you.

❖ ❖ ❖

Mortimer: What goes GNIP-GNOP, GNIP-GNOP?

Matilda: I give up.

Mortimer: A ping-pong ball bouncing backward.

Mortimer: What kind of keys don't open doors?
Matilda: You've got me.
Mortimer: Piano keys.

Mortimer: What cattle follow you wherever you go?
Matilda: My mind is a blank.
Mortimer: Your calves.

Mortimer: What is the best thing to have with you when you hike in the desert?
Matilda: I have no clue.
Mortimer: A thirst-aid kit.

Mortimer: What kinds of math do owls like?
Matilda: I don't know.
Mortimer: Owl-gebra.

Mortimer: What happened when the painter threw his pictures at the art dealer?
Matilda: I can't guess.
Mortimer: The art dealer had an art attack.

Mortimer. How do you get a peanut to laugh?
Matilda: I have no idea.
Mortimer: You crack it up.

Mortimer: What is a worn-out rifle called?
Matilda: I'm blank.
Mortimer: A shotgun.

Mortimer: What did one worm say to the
other?
Matilda: You tell me.
Mortimer: I'm moving to the big apple.

41

Franky & Fanny

Franky: What dog likes to hang around
scientists?
Fanny: I have no clue.
Franky: A laboratory retriever.

Franky: What would you get if you crossed a
Martian, a skunk, and an owl?
Fanny: I don't know.
Franky: An animal that stinks to high heaven
and doesn't give a hoot.

Franky: What did the scientist get when he
crossed an egg and a soft drink?
Fanny: I can't guess.
Franky: Yolk-a-cola.

Franky: What kind of gum do chickens chew?
Fanny: I have no idea.
Franky: Chicklets.

Franky: What has bread on both sides and
  frightens easily?
Fanny: I'm blank.
Franky: A chicken sandwich.

Franky: What do computer scientists like
  with their hamburgers?
Fanny: I'm blank.
Franky: Chips.

Franky: What always follows a horse when it
  gallops?
Fanny: You tell me.
Franky: Its tail.

Franky: What is a hot dog's favorite song?
Fanny: I give up.
Franky: "Franks for the Memory."

Franky: What is the best way to talk to a hot dog?
Fanny: You've got me.
Franky: Be frank.

Franky: What do frogs wear on their feet in summer?
Fanny: My mind is a blank.
Franky: Open toad shoes.

Franky: What did the hunter say after being on safari for one week?
Fanny: I don't have the foggiest.
Franky: Safari so good.

Franky: What do dogs drink at picnics?
Fanny: I have no clue.
Franky: Pupsi-cola.

Franky: What kind of music do you hear when you throw a stone into the lake?
Fanny: I don't know.
Franky: Plunk rock.

Franky: What is green, has big eyes, and eats like a pig?
Fanny: I can't guess.
Franky: Kermit the Hog.

Franky: What would you get if you crossed some chocolate candy and a sheep?
Fanny: I have no idea.
Franky: A Hershey baa.

42

Yolanda & Yarnell

Yolanda: What do cows give after an
  earthquake?
Yarnell: I have no clue.
Yolanda: Milk shakes.

Yolanda: What was the plumber doing in the
  operating room?
Yarnell: I don't know.
Yolanda: He was a drain surgeon.

Yolanda: What would you have if cattle from
  different farms fought each other?
Yarnell: I can't guess.
Yolanda: *Steer Wars.*

Yolanda: What game is dangerous to your
mental health?
Yarnell: I have no idea.
Yolanda: Marbles—if you lose them.

Yolanda: What music do cows like to
dance to?
Yarnell: I'm blank.
Yolanda: Cow-lypso (calypso) music.

Yolanda: What do doctors give elephants to
calm them down?
Yarnell: You tell me.
Yolanda: Trunk-quilizers.

Yolanda: What is the most important use for
an elephant's skin?
Yarnell: I give up.
Yolanda: To keep the elephant together.

Yolanda: What is a foot doctor's favorite song?
Yarnell: You've got me.
Yolanda: "There's No Business Like Toe
Business."

Yolanda: What smells good and rides a horse?
Yarnell: My mind is a blank.
Yolanda: The Cologne Ranger.

Yolanda: What do cheerleaders have for
    breakfast?
Yarnell: I don't have the foggiest.
Yolanda: Cheer-ios.

Yolanda: What is the hardest animal to ride
    bareback?
Yarnell: I have no clue.
Yolanda: A porcupine.

Yolanda: What does a sheep say when it has
    problems?
Yarnell: I don't know.
Yolanda: Where there's a wool, there's a way.

Yolanda: What is the best thing to do if a
    dinosaur charges you?
Yarnell: I can't guess.
Yolanda: Pay him.

Yolanda: What would you get if you crossed
the road with a bag of money?
Yarnell: I have no idea.
Yolanda: Mugged!

Yolanda: What should you wear when you are
feeling sad?
Yarnell: I'm blank.
Yolanda: Blue jeans.

43

Carie & Harry

Carie: Who is the meanest goat in the West?
Harry: I have no clue.
Carie: Billy the Kid.

❖ ❖ ❖

Carie: How do you fix a torn teepee?
Harry: I don't know.
Carie: Apache here, Apache there.

❖ ❖ ❖

Carie: Where do pigs park?
Harry: I can't guess.
Carie: In porking lots.

Carie: How do rabbits travel?
Harry: I have no idea.
Carie: By hareplane.

Carie: Who is boss in the dairy?
Harry: I'm blank.
Carie: The big cheese.

Carie: How can you tell if there is an elephant
 in your bathtub?
Harry: You tell me.
Carie: It's hard to close the shower curtain.

Carie: Which pilgrim refused to attend the
 first Thanksgiving?
Harry: I give up.
Carie: Captain Miles Standoffish.

Carie: Where do great dragon football
 players go?
Harry: You've got me.
Carie: To the Hall of Flame.

Carie: Who are the happiest people at a
football game?
Harry: My mind is a blank.
Carie: The cheerleaders.

Carie: Where can you find out more about
chickens?
Harry: I don't have the foggiest.
Carie: In a hen-cyclopedia.

Carie: Which way did the thief go when he
stole the computer?
Harry: I have no clue.
Carie: Data-way.

Carie: Where do you go after you've jogged
around a ship ten times?
Harry: I don't know.
Carie: To the poop deck.

Carie: Where do scientists get magnets?
Harry: I can't guess.
Carie: They grow them in magnetic fields.

Carie: Which part of a horse is the most
     important?
Harry: I have no idea.
Carie: The mane part.

Carie: Where does Lassie go on vacation?
Harry: I'm blank.
Carie: Collie-fornia.

Other Books by Bob Phillips

For information on how to purchase any of the above books, contact
your local bookstore or send a self-addressed stamped envelope to:
Family Services
P.O.Box 9363
Fresno, CA 93702

For information on how to purchase other books and
tapes by Steve Russo, as well as information on the
Real Answers radio program, school assemblies, and
crusades, contact:

Real Answers with Steve Russo
P.O. Box 1549
Ontario, CA 91762
(909) 466-7060
Fax: (909) 466-7056